TO THE LIMIT

Fantastically Fast Cars

First published in 2014 by Franklin Watts

Franklin Watts
338 Euston Road
London NW1 3BH

Franklin Watts Australia
Level 17/207 Kent Street
Sydney, NSW 2000

Produced for Franklin Watts by White-Thomson Publishing Ltd

www.wtpub.co.uk
+44 (0) 843 208 7460

Edited and designed by Paul Manning

A CIP catalogue record for this book is available from the British Library.

Dewey no: 629.2'221
Hardback ISBN: 978 1 4451 3419 2
Library eBook ISBN: 978 1 4451 3600 4

Printed in China

Franklin Watts is a division of Hachette Children's Books,
an Hachette UK company.
www.hachette.co.uk

Picture credits:
Front cover, courtesy Bloodhound SSC; 3, 5, Getty/Clive Mason; 6, Corbis/Walter
G. Arce/Icon SMI; 7, Corbis/Library of Congress; 8, Shutterstock/Maksim Toome;
8 (inset), Shutterstock/Brandon Parry; 9, Shutterstock/Reha Mark; 10, Corbis/Lor; 11,
Universal/TempSport/Corbis; 12, Auto-imagery; 13, courtesy Shirley Muldowney; 14,
Shutterstock/Luis Louro; 15, Corbis/Yves Forestier; 16, Shutterstock/James Pierce; 16,
Corbis/Russell LaBounty/ASP Inc/Icon SMI; 17, Tim Wohlford; 17, Shutterstock/John J.
Klaiber Jr; 18, courtesy Bloodhound SSC; 19, Skyscan/Corbis; 20, 21, Courtesy Adam
Kirley; 22, Shutterstock/ Jack Dagley Photography; 23, Corbis/Yasukawa; Mitsu; 24,
Shutterstock/Greg Kieca; 25, Corbis/Alessandro Biachi/Pool; 26, courtesy World First;
27 (top) ESA / Alpha Centauri Nuon Solar Racing Team; (centre), Courtesy Green GT;
27 (bottom), Courtesy BMW.

Hey there! Before reading this book, it's really important for you to know
that the fast cars and racing shown in it are meant for you to enjoy reading
and for no other purpose. The activities depicted are really dangerous; trying
to do them could hurt or even kill people. They should only be done by
professionals who have had a lot of training and, even then, they are still
really dangerous and can cause injury. So we don't encourage you to try
any of these activities. Just enjoy the read!

Contents

Dirt Track Racers

Stock car racing is rough, tough and dangerous.
It's also great fun to watch, as cars smash into
each other and spin off the track. Where DID
they learn to drive like that?

⬥ Sparks fly, rubber burns and
cars hurtle through the air
as NASCAR racers jockey for
position during a race in
Alabama in the USA.

Stock car racing in the USA goes back to the Prohibition Era of the 1920s, when bootleggers honed their driving skills in nightly games of cat and mouse with the law.

Picture the scene. In the dead of night, men are loading crates of illegal whisky into a car on a small farm in the Appalachian Mountains. The driver turns the key and the engine roars into life. 'Drive carefully, Sam,' laughs one of the men.

Dodging and weaving

A few miles down the road a police car siren pierces the night. Sam's car is small, but after the work he's done on the engine, it's fast. For half an hour, the two cars dodge and weave along the twisty mountain roads.

As he turns a corner, Sam yanks back the handbrake and his car spins around. The police car tries the same stunt – and crashes into a ditch! With a mock wave, Sam speeds off in a cloud of dust.

Driving skills

Next Saturday, Sam is back at the wheel. He lines up alongside the other stock cars on the dirt track. Now's his chance to show the other bootleggers who's boss. All those tricks he's learned running from the police will come in useful!

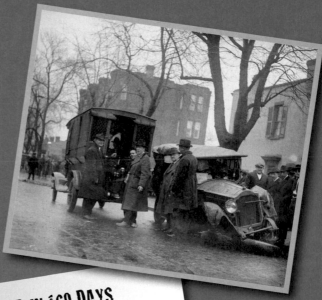

▼ *A gang of bootleggers are bundled into a police van after their car is wrecked in a chase through the streets of Chicago.*

AROUND THE WORLD IN 169 DAYS

Early car races were often marathon adventures. In 1908, The New York Times challenged drivers to race from New York to Paris across three continents – a distance of some 35,000 km. The winning car had a top speed of just 100 kph. It finished in 169 days, 26 days ahead of its nearest rival. As the race has never been repeated, the record still stands!

The Mid Night Club

In the 1990s, the Mid Night Club was the most famous illegal street racing gang in the world. Along with other Japanese street racers, its members invented 'drift racing' – hurling cars round bends in a controlled skid or slide.

Drift racing began in the 1960s with daredevil contests between rival gangs on the streets of Yokohama in Japan. Now it is a popular motor sport all round the world.

It took six simple steps to join the Mid Night Club.

1 Get a car with a top speed of 320 kph or over. Powerful engines cost money. One 'hashiriya', or street racer, spent over $2 million rebuilding his Porsche 911.

2 Obey the rules. There are only about 30 members at a time. New members become apprentices for a year, but only 1 in 10 becomes a full member. Secrecy is vital.

3 Know the time and place. The gang meets at a petrol station outside Yokohama city at midnight. Races often take place along circular motorways like the Shuto Expressway between Yokohama and Tokyo.

4 Watch out for police! As well as patrol cars, there are lots of speed traps and cameras to avoid. Some racers have number plates that rotate to hide their identity. Others paint their cars with a spray that scrambles speed-trap radars.

5 Be good – very good. Imagine slamming on the brakes on a wet road. The back of the car swings right around. That's what drift racing is all about.

6 Drive safely! You'll get thrown out if you put others at risk. In 1999, the Club broke up after an accident in which one biker died and six ended up in hospital.

LIVES ON THE LINE

Street racing is a deadly game. On 25 September 2007, US high school student Gavin Simcoe bragged to his friends, 'My car can beat yours!' Soon they were racing down a two-lane road. Out of the blue, Gavin saw headlights as a car pulled out of a driveway. He swerved and his car flipped over. Gavin was lucky to escape with a few scratches and bruises. But each year many others end up losing limbs – or lives.

A handbrake turn is the fastest, easiest and most dangerous way to make a car drift. Skilled drivers use a range of techniques and are awarded points by judges.

Drive Till You Drop

Sensible motorists take a break every couple of hours to avoid getting tired. But there's nothing sensible about the gruelling 24-hour car race that takes place each year in Le Mans, France.

▼ *Night falls but the race goes on. After driving for hours at speeds of up to 400 kph, a driver makes a night-time pit stop during the 2007 Le Mans 24-hour race.*

Your challenge: survive the Le Mans 24-hour race. This time it's not about being the first to cross the finishing line. The winning team is the one whose car completes the most laps in 24 hours.

Le Mans race cars have to be tough and reliable. Before the big day, mechanics take apart and clean the cars. Every last part is checked to make sure it will stand up to 24 hours of racing.

Driving solo

The race dates back to 1923. In the early days, some drivers drove the whole race on their own. But in 1955, solo driver Pierre Levegh killed himself and 80 spectators when he crashed. Since then, drivers have raced in teams.

You must be super-fit to drive at Le Mans. It takes strength to cope with hours of bumping and banging from the car. You'll need to drink lots of water. It can get pretty hot wearing several layers of fireproof clothing. You'll sweat so much you can lose up to 4 kg in weight during the race.

On the podium

The winning car can cover over 375 laps. If you make it onto the winner's podium, remember to spray fizzy champagne over the crowd! This tradition was started by Dan Gurney when he won Le Mans in 1967.

COOL START!

In the past, the Le Mans race started with drivers running across the track and jumping into their cars before driving away. But in 1969, rookie Jacky Ickx thought the start was too dangerous, so he slowly walked across to his car. A rival car almost ran him down. But Jacky coolly took the time to fasten his safety belt before pulling away. He went on to win the race!

▲ Drivers sprint to their cars at the start of the Le Mans 24-hour race, June 1958.

Rockets on Wheels

Drag racing takes guts. You strap yourself into a seven metre-long car that looks like a rocket on wheels. After a tyre-scorching start, you hurtle down a 400-metre strip at a speed of over 500 kph.

▼ In drag racing, drivers compete to be the first to cross a finish line, usually from a standing start. The sport first became popular in the USA after the Second World War, but races are now held at dragstrips all over the world.

▶ Champion drag-racer Shirley Muldowney roars into action at Joliet, Illinois in 2003.

Motor sport doesn't get louder or faster than drag racing. Yet Shirley Muldowney battled against all the odds to make it to the top. 'I love drag racing', she once said. 'And I love beating the boys!'

▶ Shirley Muldowney, 'First Lady of Drag Racing'.

Early on, Shirley wasn't taken seriously by the male drivers. But soon she was competing in races – and winning! When the GO! sign lit up, Shirley always reacted first. In a race lasting just five seconds, a quick start is everything.

Narrow escape

During one race, the brakes in Shirley's car failed. Though her parachute opened, her car just kept on going. It crashed through a fence and ploughed into a wood. It was so dark, Shirley couldn't see her hand in front of her. All she could hear was the branches going WHOOOSH! past her head. Finally the car shuddered to a halt. It was a close call.

A true champion

Later, Shirley drove Funny Cars (see panel). Four of them caught fire! She swore never to race in them again. But it didn't stop her realising her dream. She became the first woman to drive the very fastest dragsters, Top Fuel cars, winning the Top Fuel championship in 1977, 1980 and 1982. She even set a new speed record – at the age of 58!

DID YOU KNOW?

* A Top Fuel Dragster can reach speeds of 530 kph and accelerates faster than a jet fighter.
* A 'Funny Car' looks like an ordinary car, but has huge rear tyres for a super-quick racing start.
* Drag racers make the car wheels spin at the start of a race. Known as 'laying rubber', this leaves a sticky coating on the track that gives the tyres more grip.

Tough Going

The Paris–Dakar Rally is one of the greatest adventures on Earth. For two weeks, drivers race for more than 10,000 kilometres across deserts and mountains. More than a race, it's about staying alive!

▼ Described by its founder Thierry Sabine as 'a challenge for those who go; a dream for those who stay behind', the Paris–Dakar Rally is a supreme test of off-road driving and navigation skills.

BUILT FOR SURVIVAL

A rally car racing across desert terrain has to cope with all the rocks and bumps that a desert can throw at it. The tyres often have a chunky pattern for extra grip. Sand is another big problem – it gets everywhere and can quickly destroy an engine.

The man who first came up with the idea for a race from Paris, France, to Dakar in Senegal, West Africa, was Frenchman Thierry Sabine. In 1977, he lost his way during a motorbike race across the vast Sahara desert in northern Africa. 'No point in driving round in circles,' Thierry thought to himself. No doubt before too long somebody would come and find him.

For three days and nights he waited. And waited. Things looked bad.

A crazy plan

When the rescue team finally arrived, they found Thierry sitting on top of a large rock, deep in thought. In the desert, he'd come up with a plan for the ultimate race: the Paris–Dakar Rally!

No guts, no glory

Winning the rally depends on navigation skills, tactics and sheer bravery. In the desert there are few landmarks and it's easy to get lost. The race takes no prisoners: over the years about 60 people have died in the rally. Sadly, Thierry Sabine died in a helicopter crash during the race in 1986. But each year the thrill of taking part in this crazy adventure means that drivers keep coming back for more.

▶ *Since the first Paris–Dakar Rally in 1978, the route has often changed. This map shows the 2010 route through Argentina and Chile, via the forbidding Atacama Desert.*

▶ *Driving over rough terrain, it's easy to flip the car over on a rock. Most vehicles have a strong roll hoop or built-in roll cage to protect the drivers.*

The Rookie

Indy cars are the cream of the crop in American car racing. Winning drivers are treated like Olympic champions, but it takes something very special for a young driver, or 'rookie', to win over the crowd.

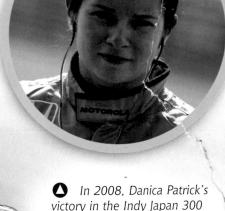

⬥ In 2008, Danica Patrick's victory in the Indy Japan 300 made her the first woman ever to win an Indy race. As well as being a top racing driver, Danica now has a thriving career as a model and TV personality.

FEEL THE G-FORCE!

When racing drivers corner at speed, they are pushed sideways in the opposite direction to the bend by a strong force known as the G-force. One 'G' is equal to the force of gravity. In 2001, officials in Texas cancelled a race because drivers were becoming dizzy. The tight turns were creating a 5G force – the equivalent of a 30 kg weight pushing at their head!

Danica Patrick began racing go-karts aged 10, along with her younger sister. Though her sister got bored with it, Danica was a natural and was soon winning races. At 16, she dropped out of school in the US and moved to England to focus on racing. It was a big gamble, but it paid off and Danica worked her way to the top.

In May 2005, Danica's big day arrived – her first appearance in the Indy 500 championship. She had been driving well during practice and decided to go for bust during her first qualifying lap. Danica roared into the first corner. But something wasn't right. The back of the car began to skate towards the wall.

Keeping her nerve

Most drivers would have taken their foot off the accelerator and let the car spin into the wall. But gutsy Danica kept her foot down. Gritting her teeth, she brought the car under control. Fellow drivers watching from the pits gasped as the car made it through the turn.

Though her error lost her first place on the starting grid, Danica's brilliant driving had already made her a legend.

▼ *Danica Patrick competing in the IndyCar series, and (right) after qualifying for the 2007 Indianapolis 500 in the USA.*

Supersonic Speedster

The latest supersonic car, the British-built *Bloodhound*, is capable of dizzying speeds. But the record-breaking success story of the British supersonic team began more than a decade ago in the deserts of Nevada in the western USA…

Combustion chamber 4.2 metres long

Driver's cockpit

Titanium wheels will be subjected to 50,000g at maximum speeds

▲ Powered by the most advanced hybrid rocket motor ever built in the UK, the Bloodhound *supersonic car is* designed to travel at up to 1,600 kph. At that speed, the aerodynamic forces acting on the car are huge.

HIT THE BRAKES!

How do you stop a car as fast as the Bloodhound? First, take your foot off the accelerator. At 1,200 kph, flaps known as airbrakes slow the car down. At 950 kph, two parachutes open. At 400 kph, it's finally safe to apply the wheel brakes. Phew! Now the driver can relax!

September 1997: the British *Thrust* Supersonic Car (SSC) team arrives in the Black Rock Desert in Nevada, USA. The rival *Spirit of America* team are waiting for them. The race is on to be the first to drive a car at the speed of sound.

The *Spirit of America* starts well, but the US team's hopes are dashed when their car's turbojet engine is hit by a lump of flying rock. A few days later *Thrust* SSC sets a new land speed record. So far, so good for the British team.

A monster ride

Two weeks later, *Thrust* SSC is edging closer and closer to breaking the sound barrier. Ahead of the car a giant shockwave forms, lifting a huge layer of dust from the desert.

Breaking the sound barrier

On the morning of 15 October, driver Andy Green is feeling confident. Around 9 am, the call goes out: 'All stations stand by. SSC engine start.'

The car streaks across the desert. It seems to be making no noise – but that's because it's travelling faster than the sound from its own exhaust!

The officials check their stopwatches. The first run is on target.

Now for the return run. *Thrust* hurtles down the track at a blistering speed. As it breaks through the sound barrier, two loud booms echo off the distant hills. *Thrust* SSC has set the world's first ever supersonic World Land Speed Record, with an incredible speed of 1,233 kph!

▼ Driver Andy Green, with Thrust SSC, the first land vehicle to break the sound barrier.

Stunt Driving

Stunt drivers perform every feat you can imagine, from tyre-screeching turns to death-defying jumps. But only the very best get to take the wheel of James Bond's Aston Martin DBS!

⬥ In the film Casino Royale, *stunt driver Adam Kirley (left) used an air cannon behind the driver's seat to flip Bond's Aston Martin DBS in a series of spectacular rolls. Says Kirley: 'You can't help but smile, thinking you've got permission to crash a car as expensive and powerful as that!'*

HOW TO BE A STUNT DRIVER

Stunt drivers need quick wits and strong nerves. According to one: 'You can't be shy, you've got to be aggressive – and athletic, too. You'll also need professional safety awareness. The greatest skill for a driver is to adapt, and adapt quickly – you don't get to do a second take in this business!'

Stunt driver Adam Kirley is one of the most sought-after names in the business with a long list of action films to his credit. But what first made him want to become a stunt driver?

'I've wanted to since I was five years old. I was brought up in the 80s, so was subjected to lots of action on TV, like *The A Team* and *Dukes Of Hazzard*. I was always very active at school, leaping around trees, so I was groomed from an early age, I guess!'

Have you ever been injured as a result of your job?

'I've had the odd few bangs, pulled ligaments, dislocated shoulder, etc., but I've never broken any bones. I've been off for a few months due to injuries, being in plaster and having physio. But within a week I'm clawing at the walls!'

Has there ever been a stunt you've refused to do?

'No, I'm open to most things within reason. If I'm unsure, then we'll just give more time for rehearsal.'

Which stunt are you most proud of?

'My favourite has to be crashing the Aston Martin at 130 kph in *Casino Royale*. I could just retire now as a happy man! I've been so fortunate even getting into the industry, but to double for James Bond is just the ultimate accolade!'

Follow That Car!

No action movie is complete without a thrilling car chase through narrow streets. But in a real-life high-speed chase, police drivers need skill, judgement – and lightning reflexes …

⬥ *Caught on camera: after a high-speed chase, a police patrol car brings a suspect vehicle to a sudden stop by ramming it from behind. Meanwhile, on the passenger side, the driver (circled) makes a hasty exit….*

⬥ *Police officers at the scene of a fatal crash. Tragically, all too many high-speed chases end in death and injury, often to innocent bystanders.*

Sitting in front of a computer screen may seem a far cry from the heart-pounding excitement of a real-life car chase. But at police training colleges in the UK and USA, new technology is transforming the way drivers are trained to cope with high-speed pursuits through busy streets.

Realistic scenes

Unfolding on screen are detailed real-life scenes filmed on actual city streets. As well as the road ahead, trainees see the car's dashboard and instruments, and the view through the rearview and wing mirrors – exactly like in a real car.

Challenges

As the scenes play out, trainees are put through a whole series of tests and challenges. How many hazards can they spot? What action will they take? How quickly can they react?

In a real chase, the answers could mean the difference between life and death. Luckily, here it's all about getting them to use their eyes and ears.

'This training system builds vital skills that are often overlooked', says training expert Bill Lewinski. 'It's far from easy, but skills soon improve with repetition.'

◀ This police patrol car is equipped with an onboard computer, enabling the driver to check details of suspicious cars within seconds on a central police database.

FOLLOW THAT TANK!

One of the strangest police chases took place in San Diego, California in 1995, when Shawn Nelson made off with a 57-tonne M60 Patton tank! Nelson led police on a 23-minute chase through the streets, ploughing through traffic lights and several cars and vans. The rampage eventually ended when the tank got stuck on a concrete barrier dividing a highway.

Accidents Can Happen

A Formula 1 race is one of the most challenging drives in the world. The cars are hi-tech wonders – but when you're driving at speeds of up to 360 kph, disaster can strike in the blink of an eye.

Formula 1 cars are marvels of engineering. Over 200 electronic sensors make 150,000 measurements each second. The seats are tough enough to stop a speeding bullet. Drivers are covered head-to-toe in fireproof layers. But you can't be too careful…

SAFETY FIRST

All Formula 1 cars must meet strict safety requirements, and crash helmets have been compulsory since 1953. A modern F1 helmet must be supremely light – around 1.2 kg – and as strong as possible to absorb impacts and protect the driver during a crash.

▶ Modern carbon-fibre crash-helmets are tested to destruction. A top-quality racing helmet like this can cost anything up to $20,000.

It's the Hungarian Grand Prix in July 2009. Brazilian driver Felipe Massa is on his final qualifying lap. Though he's slowing into a corner, the car is still travelling at 250 kph. Suddenly it swerves off the track and crashes into the safety wall of tyres. The front of the car is shredded, with both tyres gone and the front nose open. *What happened?*

The flying spring

At first people wonder if it's a beer can thrown from the crowd – but no: it's a freak accident. A spring from the car in front came loose and went bouncing down the track. Though it weighed less than a kilo, it smashed into the front of Felipe's helmet at over 150 kph.

The force was so hard it ripped away his visor and left a fist-sized dent in his helmet. Felipe was knocked out for about two seconds and had a bad gash to his forehead. He was helped from his car, then helicoptered to hospital. Luckily, after a narrow escape from death, Massa went on to make a full recovery.

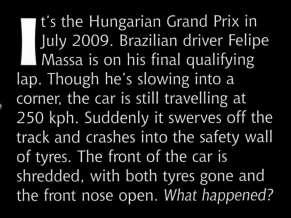 *Felipe Massa, wearing the helmet that almost certainly saved his life.*

Racing Green

Car designers are used to coming up with new ideas for making cars bigger and faster. But worries about the pollution from petrol engines may see some very different racing cars in the future…

Scientists at the University of Warwick in the UK have designed and built a Formula 3 racing car that runs entirely on vegetable oils and chocolate waste! The team behind the WorldFirst car hope that it will reach speeds of 230 kph on a racetrack.

▼ *Could 'green' motorsport really work? Yes, according to the designers of this amazing sustainable racing car.*

Steering wheel: polymer derived from carrot fibre

Damper hatch: recycled carbon fibre

Radiators: covered with a catalyst that converts ozone to oxygen

Front wing end plate: potato starch core and flax fibre shell

Running on sunshine

The record-breaking *Nuna 2* (right) moves silently and smoothly along the road, hugging the ground like a low-flying pancake. Nuna 2's shape isn't the only unusual thing about it – it runs on nothing but sunshine! Built from space-age materials, its top speed of 140 kph wouldn't scare a Formula 1 driver, but in the future, who knows how fast solar cars will go?

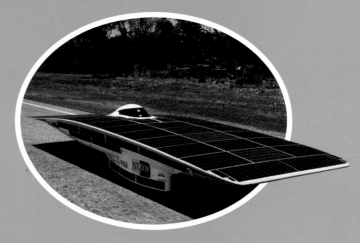

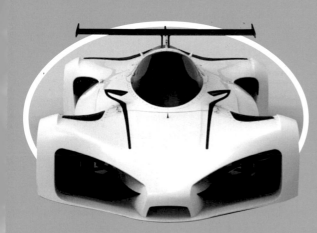

Shhh! It's electric!

Swiss team GreenGT plan to drive an electric car in the Le Mans 24-hour race (*see page 10*). The car (*left*) will be powered by two water-cooled electric motors, giving a top speed of 275 kph. Motor sports fans may miss the ear-pounding noise of the big race: those electric engines will be as quiet as a whisper!

HYBRID HEAVEN

This BMW hybrid sports car runs on a mixture of diesel and electric power, combining high performance with drastically reduced fuel consumption and emissions. Will it change the face of motoring forever?

🔻 *BMW's 356 hp diesel-electric hybrid. The sports car of the near future?*

Have You Got What It Takes?

Could you compete with the likes of Sebastian Vettel and Lewis Hamilton? Try this easy-to-answer quiz.

1 You're getting ready for a big race. Do you:
  a Chat to your mates.
  b Stay focused, memorise every bend in the course, and visualise the perfect lap.
  c Chew your nails off when you think about the dangers.

2 It is time to get suited up. What will work best?
  a A comfy tracksuit with 'go-faster' stripes.
  b A fireproof suit that covers your whole body, but thin so you don't get too hot and sweaty.
  c A thick padded suit so you won't feel the bumps on the way round.

3 You are on the grid and ready to go. What's the best way to get a good start?
  a Jam your foot on the accelerator and hope for the best.
  b Ensure your wheels are straight, release the clutch slowly but firmly, while squeezing on the power.
  c Take it nice and easy. What's the rush?

4 What is the best way to take a corner?
  a Hug the inside of the track, slam on the brakes at the last minute and spin the steering wheel.
  b Approach the corner as wide as possible, straighten the car out early and get the power on for a high-speed exit.
  c Hit the brakes early – you don't want to spin out of control.

5 You can see someone catching up in your mirrors. Do you:
  a Wait for them to pull alongside then force them off the track.
  b Block their way past, without being too aggressive.
  c Wave them through with a cheery smile.

CHECK YOUR SCORE

Mostly a's You are obviously full of confidence, but you could be a danger to yourself and everyone else on the track!

Mostly b's Excellent – you have the right attitude to be a racing driver.

Mostly c's You are probably far too sensible and relaxed to be a racing driver. If you want the thrills without the spills, why not try a computer game?

Glossary

accolade praise for doing something

aerodynamic to do with the way air flows around a moving object

apprentice somebody who is learning a skill or trade

bootlegging making, transporting and/or selling alcohol illegally

carbon-fibre type of strong lightweight material

catalyst substance that speeds up the process of chemical change

dashboard part of a car where instruments such as speedometer and fuel gauge are displayed

database way of storing and analysing information on a computer

dislocated pushed out of position

dragster type of car used for drag racing

dragstrip straight track for drag racing, usually 400 metres long

hybrid car that uses a mixture of fuels

Indy type of racing for open-wheel cars, i.e. cars with the wheels positioned outside the main car body

ligament tissue that connects bones

marathon a very long type of race

navigation finding your way from place to place

physio treatment for bone or muscle injuries

pit-stop when a racing car stops for refuelling

podium a platform where the winners of a race receive their prize

polymer material made up of many similar, smaller parts chemically linked to one another

Prohibition period in the 1920s and 1930s when alcohol was illegal in the USA

rampage when a person rushes around in a violent or uncontrolled way

roll hoop protective device inside a car

rookie inexperienced person

sensor type of measuring device

shockwave a wave of energy that travels outwards from a fast-moving object

sound barrier point at which a vehicle or aircraft starts to travel faster than the speed of sound

sprint to run fast

supersonic faster than the speed of sound

turbojet type of engine used in supersonic cars

visor part of a helmet that protects the wearer's eyes

Websites

www.formula1.com
Find out the latest news about Formula 1 motor-racing.

http://auto.howstuffworks.com/auto-racing/nascar/
A great site about NASCAR and stock car racing.

www.thrustssc.com
All about land-speed record-breaker *Thrust* SSC and its follow-up, *Bloodhound* SSC.

Note to parents and teachers

Every effort has been made by the Publishers to ensure that the web sites in this book are suitable for children, that they are of the highest educational value, and that they contain no inappropriate or offensive material. However, because of the nature of the Internet, it is impossible to guarantee that the contents of these sites will not be altered. We strongly advise that Internet access is supervised by a responsible adult.

Index